TODAY POP GOES HOME

TODAY
POP GOES
HOME

A PLAY BY
MERLE GOOD

Good Books
Intercourse, PA 17534

Design by Dawn J. Ranck
Cover illustration by Cheryl Benner

TODAY POP GOES HOME
Copyright ©1993 by Good Books, Intercourse, PA 17534
International Standard Book Number: 1-56148-098-3
Library of Congress Card Catalog Number: 93-24453
Printed in the United States of America.

Library of Congress Cataloging-in-Publication Data
Good, Merle.
    Today Pop goes home : a play / by Merle Good.
        p. cm.
    ISBN 1-56148-098-3 : $6.95
    1. Aging parents—Drama. 2. Retirement, Places of—Drama.
I. Title.
PS3557.O48T6   1993
812'.54—dc20   93-24453
                                                  CIP

Characters

Charles Snavely, a widower in his 70s, retired, who lives in the "grandparents" end of the old farmstead

Lewis Snavely, his older son, a businessman, who lives in the main part of the old farmstead with his family

Esther Snavely, Lewis' wife

Arnie Snavely, Lewis' and Esther's oldest son, in 11th grade

Margaret Sue Snavely, their only daughter, in 9th grade

Bobby Snavely, their youngest, in 7th grade

Warren Snavely, Lewis' younger brother from Fort Wayne, a school principal

"Slick" Gehman, a real estate salesman

Setting

A stairway from the second floor of the old farm house descends upstage right, reaching a landing three steps up from the main floor just right of upstage center.

The three steps come downstage from the landing. The stage is divided into two areas: to the right of the steps, a sitting room area, and to the left, a dining room area. The sitting room may have bookshelves in the wall, a fireplace along the right wall, a sofa, a stuffed chair and a braided rug, with other furnishings such as lamps, plants, etc.

The dining room area consists of a dining table with six chairs around it. Upstage left is a small room, representing a corner of the kitchen, with a swinging door on the right end of this rectangular room. Along the upstage wall, just left of center, is a desk facing the wall, with a chair.

The wall decorations are optional with the degree of realism left to the director's taste: they can include an old wood look with draperies, wall hangings, etc. In any case, the appearance is that of a modernized old house (built in the mid-1700s).

There is a door downstage right, exiting to the outside and the other side of the house.

In summary, then, there are three exits and entrances: the stairway upstage center leading upstairs offstage right, the door into the kitchen leading to the kitchen and to the basement offstage left, and the door downstage right leading outside and to the other parts of the house.

Times

Act One

Act Two

Today Pop Goes Home

Act One, *Scene One*

(Lewis Snavely, a fair-sized man in his early forties, comes down the stairs, yawning, dressed in pajamas, bathrobe, and slippers. He pauses, glances about the dining room as though trying to remember what day it is, turns and goes toward the kitchen upstage left, pauses, turns back and goes to the desk, snaps on the desk light, opens a drawer and pulls out a file folder with some letters in it. He pulls out one of these business letters and re-reads it, walking toward the table. He stands thinking, lays down the letter, puckers his lips, yawns again, and then goes into the kitchen.

Meanwhile, Charles Snavely, his father, a medium-sized man, has entered downstage right, dressed and shaved, carrying an old shopping basket under his arm. He has been to the neighbors for the morning milk. He lifts two two-quart jars of milk out of his basket and sets them on the dining room table. He is about to carry them to the kitchen to put them into the refrigerator when he notices the letter. He picks it up, reads it, and then, hearing someone in the kitchen, lays it down quickly.)

Charles: Good morning.

Lewis: *(poking his head out of the kitchen)* Good morning, Pop.

I didn't hear you come in.

Charles: Oh, it's you, Lewis.

Lewis: Yeah. Esther's not feeling so well this morning, I'm afraid.

Charles: Again? Well, I saw the light and I thought I'd bring the milk right in.

Lewis: *(coming towards him)* Here, I'll put it in the refrigerator.

Charles: *(going to do it himself)* No, I can do it. *(He goes toward the kitchen as Lewis picks up the letter, puts it back into its file, and glances at Charles as he re-enters as if to check whether his father has seen the letter.)*

Lewis: How are things over at Hiram's?

Charles: *(chuckling)* On the verge of disaster as usual. Always seems like his cows are just about to mutiny.
(exits to kitchen)

Lewis: Old Hiram's been that way as long as I can remember. *(He puts the file away.)* Well, I guess I'll have to try to throw a little breakfast together for the kids.

Charles: *(re-entering)* I'll head back to my side of the house, Lewis. You can call me when breakfast's ready.

Lewis: Do you mind?

Charles: *(a bit baffled)* Mind? No, ah, mind, I'll just be over on my end of the house and you can call me or send one of the children over when you're ready.

Lewis: No, I meant breakfast, Pop.

Charles: Breakfast—

Lewis: Do you mind helping?

Charles: Oh, do I mind helping with breakfast! You had me confused. Ah, no, I'll be glad to help. If there's anything I can do. The older you get, the more you learn.

Lewis: Well, I can probably handle it.

Charles: Lewis, you just tell me what to do. I know you have a busy day ahead of you, so I'll do what I can.

Lewis: I'm sorry Esther can't make you a good breakfast.

Charles: Oh, that's okay. I'll manage. It's too bad she's feeling depressed again.

Lewis: *(giving Pop a quick look, then planning breakfast)* I'll get some grapefruit ready, if you set the table, Pop. I guess we'll have to make do with cereal. And coffee, of course.

Charles: Instant again?

Lewis: Yeah, I don't think the pot got fixed. I'm sorry.

Charles: That's okay, Lewis. When I eat in your house, I don't complain. *(Lewis gives Pop another glance, then goes to the cupboard for the tablecloth, handing it to Pop as he goes toward the stairs.)*

Lewis: I better call the children. (*He goes up to the landing while Pop goes over to the table, touching the table gingerly.)* Arnie! *(waits)*

Charles: *(slightly disgusted)* This table is all sticky. *(goes to the kitchen for a dishcloth, re-emerging shortly)*

Lewis: Arnie!

M. Sue: *(upstairs, offstage)* I'll call him, Daddy.

Lewis: Thank you, Margaret Sue. Make sure Bobby's up too.

M. Sue: *(offstage)* I will, Daddy.

Charles: Always hate it when the table is sticky.

Lewis: You don't want to be late for school. *(He turns to walk back to the kitchen, pausing by the table to help Charles with the tablecloth.)* Have a nice evening, Pop?

Charles: *(It's his turn for a quick look, then back to casualness.)* Last night?

Lewis: Yeah, with Sally.

Charles: You really want to know?

Lewis: Why do you think I asked?

Charles: I know why you asked.

Lewis: Pop, I just wondered if you had a nice evening.

Charles: Did you know Denise called me last week?

Lewis: Denise?

Charles: You wouldn't lie to me, would you, son? You remember your youngest sister Denise—the one who left her husband last summer?

Lewis: *(insulted)* Pop—

Charles: I mean, why else would all my children descend on me, begging me not to remarry. "Please, Pop, don't marry

Sally. Mother's only been dead for a year. It would be a disgrace!" Not just you and Esther. Not just Warren from Fort Wayne. But Denise—who didn't want anyone' advice about marriage *or* divorce—calls me from Oregon And Marian, your other sister, writes me this long letter from the Middle East—all four of you pleading in no uncertain terms against Sally.

Lewis: Pop, I didn't mean to get into an argument.

Charles: I get the feeling someone's trying to get me to break it off with Sally. *(laughs with disgust)* Someone's trying to keep me from driving a car anymore. And someone's trying to hint that I should stay to my end of the house more. Maybe I should move out, in fact. I'm just a plain-down burden.

Lewis: Please, Pop.

Charles: It's either you or Esther or both.

Lewis: *(irritated)* Pop, all I asked was, did you have a nice evening.

Charles: *(without missing a beat)* Yes, I had a nice evening. Sally cooked a casserole for supper and we took a walk afterwards and she showed me her new record player.

Lewis: *(going towards the kitchen)* I'm glad.

Charles: Where's the grapefruit?

Lewis: I'm getting it.

Charles: And I scratched the car.

Lewis: *(coming back from the kitchen without the grapefruit)* What?

Charles: Nothing serious.

Lewis: What did you say?

Charles: I said I scratched the car, Lewis. You having problems with your hearing?

Lewis: The Buick?

Charles: It's nothing much, but I thought I should tell you before you discovered it. If only my car hadn't been in the garage. I can handle it so much better.

Lewis: *(softly, incredulous)* You scratched the new Buick? *(pause)* How?

Charles: To tell you the truth, I don't know. I took Sally to the shopping center to buy a new dishpan because hers is cracked so bad she can't tape it anymore.

Lewis: And it happened there?

Charles: Must have. I said last night I'd be glad to take the station wagon.

Lewis: But how'd it happen?

Charles: I didn't really notice it until I got back here last night, Lewis. Some guy must have backed into me.

Lewis: Oh, that's just great. I was going to take these American International guys out for lunch today. In a smashed-up car!

Charles: It's not smashed-up. It's scratched.

Lewis: They're coming down from New York to make Brian and me an offer today.

Charles: I know.

Lewis: *(sighs)* Well, let's get breakfast ready. *(He turns to go into the kitchen, then turns back to Charles.)* Pop, I don't want us talking about these things in front of the children. *(An instant later Margaret Sue appears on the stairs.)*

M. Sue: *(loud, enthusiastic)* Good morning, Daddy. Hello, Grandpa. It's another fine morning, isn't it?

Lewis: Good morning, Margaret Sue.

Charles: Hello there, early riser.

Lewis: Where's Arnie?

M. Sue: Oh, he's shaving in the bathroom. It takes such a long time because he has to hunt for his whiskers. All five of them!

Lewis: Margaret Sue, would you be a good girl and get the grapefruit ready? Mother's not feeling well again this morning.

M. Sue: I know. I talked to her upstairs. I sure hope she feels well enough to iron my new shirt for the fair tonight.

Charles: Fair time again?

Lewis: I'm going up to shave.

M. Sue: Yeah, the parade's tonight. *(going out to the kitchen)*

Lewis: I guess you saw the letter from Timber Realty.

Charles: *(a bit embarrassed)* I didn't mean to. It was just lying there on the table.

M. Sue: *(re-emerging)* How many grapefruits do we need?

Lewis: I meant to tell you about it, but kept forgetting. Slick's coming over tonight.

Charles: Slick?

M. Sue: Daddy—

Lewis: Can't you count, Margaret Sue?

M. Sue: I didn't volunteer for this job. Bobby'll miss his bus if we don't hurry.

Lewis: Six.

M. Sue: Six? I thought five.

Charles: You're forgetting your mother.

M. Sue: Will she be down?

Lewis: I expect so.

M. Sue: *(sighs)* Okay, six. *(goes back to the kitchen)*

Lewis: *(looking back at Charles)* Howard Gehman's boy.

Charles: Oh, yeah—*that* fellow. Why exactly do they call him Slick?

Lewis: I think it's because of the way he combs his hair. I have a hunch, however, that he's a chip off the old block when it comes to slippery business dealings.

Charles: Slick begets Slick, huh? *(Lewis nods as Arnie comes jogging down the steps, dressed in a football sweater and jeans, punching his fists playfully at his father as he passes him.)*

Lewis: Yeah. I figured I should listen to what he has to say, but I can't take him very seriously. I'll be right down, Pop. *(He goes up the stairs. Margaret Sue re-enters, carrying*

*halves of grapefruit which she sets on the table which
Charles has been setting all this time. Arnie continues
to jog in place and execute a whole series of physical
exercise techniques including push-ups, sit-ups,
toe-tappers, and punching an imaginary punching bag.)*

Charles: What kind of cereal do we want?

M. Sue: Cornflakes.

Arnie: *(without a pause in his action)* Wheaties.

M. Sue: Cornflakes.

Charles: Okay, I'll get the Wheaties.

M. Sue: Cornflakes.

Charles: Gotta keep our football star in shape.

Bobby: *(coming down the steps, books in hand)* I want Life.

Charles: *(chuckling)* Don't we all. Good morning, Bobby. *(exits)*

M. Sue: Oh boy, what are you all dressed up for?

Bobby: They're electing today.

M. Sue: Electing what?

Bobby: Student council.

Arnie: Student council in seventh grade! Whoopee-do.

Bobby: What's wrong with that?

M. Sue: Let's hear your speech.

Arnie: Probably running against all girls.

Bobby: I am not. *(He goes to sit at the table.)*

M. Sue: I bet you are!

Bobby: I am not. *(Charles returns with both kinds of cereals.)* Where's the milk?

Charles: *(sits)* You better wait for your father.

Bobby: I'll miss my bus.

M. Sue: I'll get the milk. *(exits)*

Arnie: *(still exercising, sing-song)* Bobby wants his milk. *(sarcastic)* A real baby, running for president!

Bobby: I am not.

Arnie: Am not what?

Bobby: *(pause)* I'm not so sweaty they can smell me across the room.

Arnie: Okay, lay off.

Bobby: How come you exercise all the time? Football players are supposed to be strong jocks without all that endless sweaty exercising.

Charles: He's getting ready for the big game against the Susquehanna Bears, aren't you, Arnie?

M. Sue: *(enters)* Here's your milk. And don't forget to eat your grapefruit.

Bobby: I don't like grapefruit. Besides, it'll squirt me up.

Arnie: Ha! Big student council president says "squirt me up."

Bobby: What's wrong with that?

Arnie: It's baby talk. Besides, it sounds crude.

Bobby: It does not. I'm sure Daddy says it that way. Doesn't he, Grandpa?

Charles: You better eat, Bobby. Don't worry about squirting your shirt if you're careful. What about family worship, Margaret Sue?

Arnie: Let's skip it. I knew it would never work.

Bobby: *(between spoons)* Besides, I'm not running for president. Mr. Laruck says I should just try to get elected President can come later.

M. Sue: I'll get the Bibles. *(goes to bookshelf in living room under stairs)*

Arnie: I'm going to eat. I gotta leave for school five minutes early. *(crosses toward table)*

M. Sue: I'm going along.

Arnie: You better hurry if you are. *(He sits at the table and starts on his grapefruit.)*

Bobby: I sure hope you beat those Bears this year.

Arnie: Why don't you shut up. The game's not till Thanksgiving.

Bobby: *(as Charles stands)* Anybody could beat those Bears.

M. Sue: I'll call Daddy.

Charles: I'll get the coffee. *(goes into kitchen)*

M. Sue: Daddy.

Lewis: *(offstage)* Coming.

Bobby: Besides, girls are just as hard to beat.

Arnie: Ha! You *are* running against all girls.

Bobby: Randy Stewart's running. But girls aren't easy to beat. People pity them.

M. Sue: Do not.

Bobby: Do.

M. Sue: Do not.

Bobby: Do.

Charles: *(re-entering)* Amen.

Arnie: Which way?

Lewis: *(coming down the steps)* I'll be right there. I have to call Brian.

Arnie: Let's skip the Bible-reading.

Charles: Arnie, you should be ashamed of yourself. We all agreed to give it another try.

Arnie: Well, "we" don't have the time.

Lewis: *(dialing)* Get the Bibles ready, Margaret Sue.

M. Sue: They're on the table.

Bobby: You're squirting me.

Charles: *(not quite convinced himself)* That wasn't me.

Bobby: Yes, it was. Right on my clean shirt.

Charles: It wasn't me, Bobby.

Lewis: Brian? Lewis. Will Joe be meeting us at eleven as planned? Good. I just wanted to know if you could drive to take these men out for lunch?

Bobby: I'm going upstairs to wash it off. *(getting up)*

Arnie: Good. Don't forget your perfume. *(Bobby turns to glower at him, then runs up the stairs.)*

Lewis: It's just that we had a slight mishap with my car and I'd prefer not to drive. Okay. See you at the office. Bye.

Arnie: What happened to the car?

Lewis: *(coming to the table)* Where's Bobby?

M. Sue: Upstairs.

Arnie: What happened to the car?

Lewis: *(with a glance at Pop, then calling Bobby)* Bobby! *(to Arnie, offhand)* Oh, nothing much.

Arnie: *(following the glance)* Did you have an accident again, Grandpa?

Charles: Again?

Arnie: You almost rolled your Plymouth on the river road last summer.

Charles: Oh, that. A little exaggerated, I'm afraid.

M. Sue: *(teasing)* Another heavy date, Grandpa?

Lewis: Hey, watch your mouth, young lady. Get your Bibles ready. What's the scripture this morning? *(he sits)* Bobby!

Arnie: I really oughta be going, Daddy.

Lewis: *(brusque)* You wait. We're going to have family worship if it kills us.

M. Sue: That's an awful thing to say.

Charles: Yes, it was.

Lewis: *(appearing frustrated)* I'm sorry it sounded that way. Bobby!

Charles: 1 Corinthians 13:4-10.

Bobby: *(coming down the steps)* I'll miss the bus!

Lewis: Sit down.

M. Sue: I memorized that last year.

Charles: I remember, Margaret Sue.

Lewis: *(glancing around as Bobby sits down)* Okay, now, let's quiet down. Margaret Sue, will you read?

Charles: Maybe she can do it by memory.

Arnie: That'll take too long. *(He continues to nibble on some bread.)*

Charles: How about if I read every other verse, Margaret Sue. Would that help you?

M. Sue: Use King James. *(Charles checks his Bible's cover to verify the version.)*

Bobby: Why?

M. Sue: Cause Daddy wants us to memorize from it.

Lewis: Let's not go over that again!

Charles: *(He clears his throat as he prepares to read; Arnie is still nibbling; Charles reads with feeling.)* Charity suffereth long and is kind; charity envieth not; charity vaunteth not itself, is not puffed up.

M. Sue: *(by memory)* Doth not behave—Doth not behave itself *(pause)*

Charles: Unseemly—

M. Sue: I'll get it if you let me.

Arnie: You better hurry.

Lewis: Arnie.

M. Sue: Doth not behave itself unseemly;—seeketh not her own—ah—seeketh not her own,—ah—is not easily provoked—

Charles: Right.

M. Sue: Thinketh no evil.

Charles: Rejoiceth not in iniquity but rejoiceth in the truth.

M. Sue: Beareth all things, believeth all things, hopeth all things, endureth all things (*Esther is coming down the steps slowly, in her bathrobe, looking a bit unhappy and disheveled.*)

Charles: (*without seeing Esther*) Charity never faileth; but whether there be prophecies, they shall fail (*his voice is fervent—the words have special feeling for him*); whether there be tongues, they shall cease—(*sees Esther and pauses as she comes to her place at the table, everyone watching her silently*)—whether there be knowledge, it shall vanish away.

Lewis: Good morning, honey. (*She sits, merely nodding faintly.*)

M. Sue: (*pausing to look at her mother, then continuing*) For we know in part, and we prophesy in part.

Charles: But when that which is perfect is come, then that which is in part shall be done away. (*He looks at Lewis to indicate that that's the end of the reading.*)

Lewis: (*solemnly*) Bobby, will you pray?

Bobby: *(bowing his head, as the others follow)* Thank you for this day, Lord. Help me to be an example today. I pray, if it's your will, that I may win the election today. And be with Arnie and the team, and with Margaret Sue, too. Bless Daddy and Mother today. And Grandpa, too. Amen. *(He whips his head up from prayer and jumps up from the table all in one continuous action.)* I sure hope I don't miss my bus. *(He runs over to pick up his books and runs out downstage right as Arnie gets up from the table.)*

Arnie: Margaret Sue, are you ready?

M. Sue: In a minute.

Arnie: You better wait for the bus.

M. Sue: No, I'm going with you. I gotta get my violin. Then I'm ready. *(She goes upstairs.)*

Charles: *(humored)* Arnie, you realize you've got two different kinds of socks on?

Arnie: Do I? *(checks his feet)*

Charles: *(chuckling)* Looks sorta funny.

Arnie: *(irritated)* Like the Buick?

Charles: Pardon?

Arnie: Beginners should stick to the pickup, I was always told.

Charles: I'm sorry Arnie. My Plymouth is in the garage. I didn't mean anything by it. *(Esther gets up and goes to the kitchen, almost as though to avoid the conflict.)*

Lewis: Arnie, I don't want you talking to Pop that way.

M. Sue: *(coming down the steps with her violin)* Let's go.

Arnie: *(looking at his father and grandfather, beginning to say something, then thinking better of it)* See you.

Lewis: Have a good day now. *(Arnie nods as he grabs a single book and his gym bag and strides out downstage, pausing to look back as Margaret Sue speaks.)*

M. Sue: You too, Daddy. Goodbye, Grandpa. *(Charles nods, as she raises her voice, calling.)* Goodbye, Mother.

Esther: *(appearing from the kitchen)* Goodbye, children. Drive carefully. *(She appears withdrawn and hesitant.)*

M. Sue: We will. *(Arnie and Margaret Sue exit. Lewis stands up, having barely sipped his coffee, crosses to kiss Esther on the cheek as Charles sits eating his grapefruit.)*

Lewis: Feeling better?

Esther: Some.

Lewis: Why don't you have some breakfast?

Esther: *(looping her arm around Lewis)* I will if you will.

Lewis: Honey, I can't. I have to get to the office. Today's the big day.

Esther: But you should eat.

Lewis: *(pulling away)* I'll have a big lunch. Will you be okay today?

Esther: Sure.

Lewis: Come on, sit at the table and have a grapefruit.

Esther: *(suddenly)* You probably didn't make any eggs?

Lewis: No, I'm sorry I didn't. *(Charles turns his head at the mention of eggs, obviously a bit amazed at her nerve in suggesting something he thinks she should have prepared herself. Then he goes back to eating.)*

Esther: That's okay. Maybe I can make some later. Would you like some eggs, Pop?

Charles: *(cautious)* You know I like eggs, Esther. But I can make do with what's on the table.

Esther: Oh, and I promised you hot oatmeal this morning! *(Her voice changes tones abruptly, giving us the feeling of an emotional woman, not deranged, not malicious, but warm, tender, and volatile.)* I'm really sorry.

Lewis: I'll get my coat—I must have left it upstairs.

Esther: Okay. I think I might try one of these grapefruits. *(Lewis goes upstairs as she sits at the table.)* Oh, Lewis, you haven't eaten anything.

Charles: I guess he's all worked up about these New York fellows.

Esther: American International.

Charles: Are he and Brian really going to sell H & S to them?

Esther: You know as much as I do, I guess. When Lewis said he wanted to quit, Brian decided to sell out. *(spooning out grapefruit)* Oh, excuse me, did I squirt you, Pop? *(He is wiping his forehead, which is wrinkled with perturbation.)* Sorry. Seems like the grapefruit I buy always squirt so much.

Charles: *(grimaces)* It's okay, Esther. You know, I remember when Lewis began working for H & S years ago. I got him the job. Abe started the business in a small way in the '40s. I started working with him about ten years later when the farm wasn't doing so good.

Esther: When H & S wasn't doing so good, either, right?

Charles: That's when I scraped some money together and we formed a partnership—Horning and Snavely—H & S. I always liked to sell farm equipment. *(Lewis comes back down the stairs, watching the two of them.)*

Esther: You as well as bailed out Abe Horning, isn't that right? *(notices Lewis)* Pop's giving me a history lesson on H &

Charles: I didn't say a word about their new compulsory retirement policy!

Lewis: You sure like to bring up the sore points, don't you Pop!

Esther: *(with an edge)* He never stops.

Lewis: Listen, you two have all day to reminisce. I gotta go. *(to Esther)* You okay, Esther?

Esther: I'll survive.

Lewis: *(concerned)* Shall I call Dr. Elder?

Esther: No, no. Don't bother the poor man. *(She turns in her chair as though to plead with him.)* Please.

Lewis: Okay, honey. I'll call you as soon as I know if we have a deal. Then I can finally start slowing down. *(pats her hand affectionately)* Hang in there. *(He bends down and kisses her on the forehead. Then he walks over toward his briefcase, pausing to look back at his father.)* Don't worry about the car. I'll get it fixed. See you tonight.

Charles: I'm sorry. I'll pay for it.

Lewis: Don't worry, Pop. We'll talk about it later. *(He takes his briefcase and goes to leave downstage right.)* Have a nice day, both of you. *(He goes out, and the mood in the house changes. It is more lonely, more fragile, more stark. Charles finishes his cereal while Esther sips her coffee, staring out at the day, thinking. After a long silence, Charles speaks.)*

Charles: Is he really going to quit his job?

Esther: Lewis keeps his promises. He does that.

Charles: But what's he going to do if he doesn't work at H & S? You two can't live on nothing, and *you* certainly don't bring home the bacon.

Esther: *(flares)* Is that right? Well, well. How can I go get a job when I have you to take care of?

Charles: *(laughs)* I can take care of myself.

Esther: Is that a guarantee?

Charles: I could still be working at H & S if they hadn't forced me to retire last year. Brian did it. His father's gone, so he couldn't stand two Snavelys around.

Esther: Can you blame him?

Charles: *(ignoring her)* Brian never learned to work. He never had the touch for business. Oh, he can talk big and can walk big. But without Lewis, that business would have gone down the tubes.

Esther: So what else is new! You saved Abe—and Lewis saved Brian. Funny thing is, the Hornings still own 90% of H & S. *(laughs)* Lewis works himself crazy, solves the

problems and minds the store while Brian drives his big
car and wears his white shoes! And we own a measly 10'

Charles: *(irritated)* Don't bring that up again.

Esther: I didn't bring up anything. I just stated some facts.
(pause) What did Lewis say about the Buick?

Charles: *(looks at her cautiously, does not want to upset her)*
Esther, maybe if you're not feeling too well today—
(She gives him a look he knows he must answer.)—It got
scratched last night.

Esther: Last night? How?

Charles: I don't know.

Esther: Oh, you were out with Sally again? *(He nods.)* Did you
roll it?

Charles: No, no, nothing like that, Esther. It's just scratched along
the driver's side. Must have happened at the shop—

Esther: Shopping center. *(Suddenly her voice flits up into a
higher register as she tries to control her apparent anger.
She smiles all the time when she tries to control her
emotion.)* That's just great, Charles. We have a pickup,
we have Arnie's jalopy, we have a four-year-old station
wagon. And then there's this new Buick which I finally
persuaded Lewis to buy. And what do you take on a date'
We've been begging you not to drive, but, oh no, you just
must see Sally. Like some fresh high school boy you run
around with that woman, never minding what people
might say! *(She breaks into laughter as though it's funny,
then stops abruptly.)*

Charles: *(hurt)* I'm truly sorry, Esther. But it's really not my fault. I told Lewis I'd rather take the station wagon.

Esther; Oh wow! A thousand wows! Big talking, empty-headed Brian has a Cadillac *and* a Mercedes sports car. I finally talk Lewis into a new modest Buick and wouldn't you know the neighbor man who can't keep his old Plymouth fixed takes it out on a wild date and wrecks it!

Charles: *(voice raised)* It's not wrecked, it's scratched! *(pause, quietly)* He's not going to let me drive anymore, is he?

Esther: He shouldn't.

Charles: Why not? You want to chauffeur me everywhere, Esther?

Esther: *(laughs nervously)* Oh, Pop. You have a way of melting Lewis.

Charles: He's my son, isn't he?

Esther: He's always so easy on you.

Charles: I suppose you'd even take away your own father's license if you lived close enough. *(He gets up and walks downstage, sipping coffee.)*

Esther: My father's in perfect health. He doesn't have fainting spells. He's an excellent driver. And he's not one bit senile. *(She catches herself too late.)*

Charles: *(trying to act casual, but obviously scalded by the comment)* Senile? Implying what?

Esther: Oh, I'm tired of talking about it. I wish it would all go away.

Charles: I am *not* senile, Esther, and I won't have you implying that I am.

Esther: How do you know?

Charles: *(laughing)* I know!

Esther: How?

Charles: I know I'm not senile the same way—excuse my saying it, Esther, but you asked for it—the same way you know you're not—*(pauses)*

Esther: Not what?

Charles: I shouldn't have said it.

Esther: Not what? Emotionally ill?

Charles: You said it, I didn't.

Esther: That's where we're different. I admit my illness. Everyone knows I've been to Valley Vista twice in the past two years. So why should I deny it?

Charles: But no one's proved that there's anything wrong with me.

Esther; If only Buicks could talk! *(They stare at each other, then fall silent. He sips and she stares.)* Did I tell you about Ruth Burkholder and her parents? *(He doesn't respond, his back to her as he stands looking out into the audience as though studying the landscape. She doesn't seem to notice, the story cooking out of her from deep inside without her realizing why she's telling it.)* Ruth's had five children, you know. And the youngest just got married in June. She smiled when she said it, "Free, at last." All those things she wanted to do. Ruth's not an independent woman. But she just had all these things she wanted to do. Only her parents came to see her last week. "We're getting pretty old," her father says, "My driving's not so good and Mother's leg is getting worse. Could we move in with you?" *(Charles listens carefully, trying to act unaffected, but his eyes fill with tears nonetheless.)* What could Ruth say? She had those empty rooms. And she wasn't very busy. So she says "Sure, Pop, we'd be glad to have you." How could she say no? *(pause)* But what about the rest of her life? It won't get any better as her parents keep slipping. They'll become more helpless and Ruth won't have a moment free. *(She pauses, and her voice drops to a whisper.)* What about the rest of her life?

Charles: *(his tears still wet in his eyes, trying to control his voice)* Why do you tell me this story, Esther? *(without turning)*

Esther: *(innocently)* I just think it's awful sad. I always liked Ruth.

Charles: *(Suddenly angry, he strides back to the table, putting down his cup.)* May I ask you a question?

Esther: Me? *(grins, sensing his anger)* If you wish.

Charles: Why don't you just—*(gestures)* why don't you just get hold of yourself?

Esther: May I ask you a question?

Charles: Things would be so much happier around here if you just got hold of yourself and cleaned things up a little and tried to be a good wife and mother.

Esther: *(voice rising)* I said, may I ask you a question?

Charles: You didn't hear what I said, did you? *(They stare at each other for one locked angry moment.)*

Esther: Why don't you just get hold of yourself *(stands up, her voice animated and angry)*—get hold of *yourself,* Charlie, *yourself,* and things *(throws a spoon at him)*—things would be a lot happier around here. Happier! *(She sinks exhausted into her chair, fighting tears, her voice barely a whisper now.)* You can be so mean, Pop.

Charles: *(shaking his head)* It's all my fault again. *(gestures in frustration)* I'm going home.

Esther: Good!

Charles: It's only on the other end of the house!

Esther: I know. *(sighs)* I'm sorry, Pop. I really am. You won't tell Lewis, will you? I'm awful sorry.

Charles: *(with deliberate pause)* Not as long as you don't turn against me. *(He gives her a meaningful glance.)* Let's not act like children, Esther. We can get along if we just try. We Snavely's have always tried to be peace-making people, remember? *(She doesn't say anything as he pauses.)* Okay, I'll see you later. *(He goes out.)*

Esther: *(gestures feebly)* Later. *(to herself)* Welcome to another long day, Esther.

(CURTAIN)

Act One, *Scene Two*

(As curtain rises, Lewis is sprawled on the sofa in the living room, feet up on the coffee table, reading the Wall Street Journal. *Esther enters from the kitchen, taking off her apron as she enters.)*

Esther: But who is this Slick Gehman, Lewis? Why's he coming? Are you seriously thinking of selling the farm to him?

Lewis: *(without looking up)* Howard Gehman's boy. Not too bright, I always thought.

Esther: Are you?

Lewis: *(looking up)* Pardon? What did you say?

Esther: *(sits)* Are you seriously thinking of selling this place?

Lewis: Oh, I don't know. It would be very hard. Snavelys have been here for generations. No one else has ever farmed this land. But we must find a livelihood, Esther, if I quit H & S.

Esther: What would you do with the money if you sold the farm?

Lewis: *(shrugs)* We could begin a new, small enterprise of some sort. Maybe we could even start a little cottage industry here in the barn—

Esther: Are you kidding? *(laughs)* Like what? Chicken feeders, or water bowls for cows!

Lewis: I don't know. Esther, I'm bushed. Maybe we can talk about this another day.

Esther: Besides, if we start another business, it'll just be the same rat race all over again. You're so thorough, Lewis,

---

you want everything just right. Soon you'll be tied up day and night again, just like at H & S.

Lewis: You have a point there.

Esther: It *is* revenge, isn't it, Lewis?

Lewis: Revenge! What in the world are you implying?

Esther: You're trying to scare Pop away by acting like you're going to sell the farm! I know how your mind works.

Lewis: *(laughing, being careful)* Do you now? Well, why don't you give me a tour.

Esther: Hey, Lewis, don't get upset. I just don't think it's fair to pressure Pop.

Lewis: Esther, we must find a solution that'll make all of us happy. I'm going through a great deal of red tape to quit my busy schedule and be home more. But that won't necessarily mean that you and Pop will get along any better.

Esther: Will *you* be fun to grow old with? *(changing subjects)* I sure hope the kids are having a good time at the fair. The weather's nice enough.

Lewis: *(going toward the kitchen)* Yeah, maybe you and I should have gone. You want something to drink?

Esther: *(standing abruptly)* I'll get it, Lewis. I'm sorry. I didn't know you wanted something to drink. *(She crosses toward the kitchen; he stops her, turns her around, and guides her back to where she was sitting, hands her the* Wall Street Journal, *and helps her to sit while all the time she's half resisting and half enjoying it.)*

Lewis: You just sit down and relax, Esther. All I wanted was a Diet Pepsi. You want something?

Esther: No.

Lewis: You better read the *Journal* if we're going to be in business together!

Esther: Really! *(She looks at the paper as he disappears into the kitchen; she calls after him.)* Remember when we were first married and we went to the fair one night and some of those tough guys started getting fresh with me?

Lewis: (re-emerging with a glass of soda) Can you blame them?

Esther: You sure scared them. I can still picture the expression on the face of that one roughneck!

Lewis: (laughing) Yeah, that was quite the night.

Esther: *(tender, looking up at him)* You're some Snavely!

Lewis: Oh. Is that good or bad? *(crosses to sit opposite)*

Esther: All I said is—you're some Snavely.

Lewis: Thanks. We've been through a lot together.

Esther: We haven't lost each other yet, Lewis.

Lewis: *(firmly)* And we're not about to.

Esther: *(after a pause, standing suddenly, moving to table)* I'm sorry, Lewis.

Lewis: *(baffled, isn't sure he's heard)* I'm sorry.

Esther: No, I said *I'm* sorry.

Lewis: *(sitting on edge of chair)* About what, Esther?

Esther: *(her back to him)* Pop and I had another quarrel.

Lewis: Oh?

Esther: I guess I was upset about the Buick. After ordering it and waiting all those months, then Pop gets it scratched.

Lewis: I can get it fixed.

Esther: He said I couldn't be counted on to "bring home the bacon."

Lewis: He said what?

Esther: I didn't tell him I always sorta wanted a job, Lewis. Part-time someplace, nothing too difficult. But first there were the kids. Then your mother. Taking care of her was almost more than I could handle.

Lewis: It sure was more than part-time. Two and a half years. If Pop hadn't gotten so stubborn and had done more for her himself, you wouldn't have been so strapped.

Esther: Toward the end, he hardly did a thing for her.

Lewis: Charles Snavely didn't know what to do without his Elsa.

Esther: I always thought of my father-in-law as a strong man. Oh, he could be a little grouchy, but he was tough. But when your mother got cancer, he just went to pieces.

Lewis: I'm not sure he's back together yet. *(pause)* You know, it would solve a lot of problems if he got married. Do you think he might?

Esther: You think so?

Lewis: No, I said do you think so?

Esther: Marry Sally? No way.

Lewis: Why not?

Esther: He enjoys the fight more than the woman.

Lewis: The fight?

Esther: With his children. It tells him he's still alive and doing well if he can have an out-and-out conflict with all four children at the same time.

Lewis: You think he's been dating Sally just to punish us?

Esther: No, not just for that. He is lonely, too. And a little confused. He misses your mother more than we know.

Lewis: But he doesn't really love Sally?

Esther: Love her? No. Like her? Yes. In the sense that one might like any of two hundred friendly persons who happen to be nearby when you feel lonely. Personally, I like Sally myself. I think's she's a really kind person. She'd take good care of Pop. She would. Oh, she's no Elsa, but I suppose it's soon time that we all face up to the realization that Elsa's gone. And she won't be back.

Lewis: *(emotional)* You're a good woman, Esther.

Esther: *(looks at him, a bit embarrassed)* No, I feel so inadequate.

Lewis: *(shaking his head)* You're a good woman. *(They exchange a loving glance.)* So you think he won't marry her?

Esther: You sound disappointed. I didn't know that's what you wanted.

Lewis: I don't know what I want. But I'm convinced we must do something.

Esther: *(with a touch of nervousness)* Lewis, I'm sorry I'm such a problem. *(listens)* Was that a car?

Lewis: It's probably Slick Gehman. Now don't worry, Esther. I won't up and sell the farm without talking it over. I just want to hear what he has to say. Maybe it will help us to figure out what to do. *(The door opens and Arnie enters.)* Arnie?

Arnie: *(gestures)* I brought Grandpa home.

Lewis: *(surprised)* I thought he was home. Weren't you at the fair'

Arnie: He's home now. *(Lewis, ready to ask another question, catches himself, looks at Esther, then back at Arnie, waiting for Arnie to explain.)* He had another accident.

Esther: With the Buick?

Lewis: Is he hurt bad?

Arnie: Charlie Snavely doesn't get scratched! But his Plymouth looks a sight.

Esther: Plymouth?

Lewis: Pop and I picked it up after work.

Esther: Oh, I didn't realize. Are you okay, Arnie?

Arnie: Johnny Martin rushes up to me and says, "Hey, your old man made a pretty picture of Leland Miller's pickup." I says, "What, my dad?" And he says, "No, no, Charlie— your grandpa." So I went to see and sure enough—there they were. Leland had lost his temper and he told Grandpa a thing or two. And Grandpa—he didn't say a word.

Esther: Really?

Arnie: Not a word. And on the way home he was all clammed up, too, till we came in the lane. Then he says, "Lewis won't let me drive anymore, will he?"

Lewis: I better go over and see that he's okay.

Arnie: He's okay. He's just humiliated, that's all.

Esther: Where are Bobby and Margaret Sue?

Arnie: Oh, they're fine. I told them to stick with Barb and Henry Hess until I get back.

Lewis: Thanks, Arnie. You handled things very well.

Arnie: *(shrugging, but appreciating the compliment)* Hey, it's not the first time—and I'm sure it won't be the last. *(goes to leave)* I gotta say, I never saw Leland Miller so mad! He used a few words I've never heard—must have been Pennsylvania Dutch or something.

Lewis: *(chuckles)* Leland's a Dutchman, all right. And a little expressive sometimes. See you soon, Arnie.

Arnie: Don't worry, Mom. We'll all be home soon.

Esther: See you then. *(He goes out.)*

Lewis: *(crossing toward the door)* I better check out, Pop, Esther. I'll be right back.

Esther: Okay. Remember this realtor's coming.

Lewis: *(pausing by door)* You know, Esther, looking at Arnie just now reminded me of myself. My brother Warren's always talking about his "fond memories" of when we where young. Sure, Warren has fond memories—he was having a high time as pitcher on the summer ball team while I was helping care for both Grandmom and Grandpap. Why do you think we never went on family vacations when I was a teenager? Day after day up in that stuffy room where Pop now sleeps, turning

Grandmom's withering body slowly on the mattress so that her bedsores would be more bearable. And Grandpap's mind slipping more all the time. I was the oldest child and I spent as much time taking care of Grandpap and Grandmom as Pop did! Right up till the summer we got married. Some people age gracefully, I've heard. My family doesn't.

Esther: You sound angry.

Lewis: I look at Arnie and see myself. Marian, always the churchworker, was off volunteering to help the orphans and the refugees before she was through high school. And Denise—well, we never could count on Denise to be responsible, could we? Sure, Warren's glad to sit in Indiana with his fond memories while we're stuck here on the "Homeplace Nursing Home." Me? I remember Pop saying "No" to camp, "No" to a three-week hiking trip, "No" to a summer in Europe. No, No, No! "We need you here, Lewis!"

Esther: Why didn't he make Warren help?

Lewis: You tell me! I guess Pop always had a weakness for sports, just the way he's proud of Arnie now on the football team. Warren *was* a superb pitcher, and Pop didn't want to ask him to give that up. Besides, he was younger.

Esther: So you want to sell the farm to get even?

Lewis: How can you say such a thing?

Esther: I think I know you.

Lewis: Esther, you can't have it both ways. You can't say you can't bear to live next to Pop anymore—and then turn around and argue against every solution I propose! Do you want us to end up penniless so our children can fight over the privilege of taking care of us?

Esther: I know you love him, Lewis. Don't do anything you'll regret forever. Pop has always lived here. You'd be pulling him up by his roots. Like a tree that still has a lot of life in it.

Lewis: Not if he got married. *(pause, then with frustration)* Esther, you can be just as demanding as your mother sometimes.

Esther: *(laughing nervously)* Zingo! What do I demand of you, Lewis?

Lewis: I shouldn't have said it.

Esther: *(strained)* Well, I'm sorry, Lewis, if I'm demanding. I try so hard to not be a bother to you. Maybe I should just go back to Valley Vista.

Lewis: *(quickly and firmly)* No. *(pause)* After our luncheon with these New York fellows, I wanted to clear out my mind a little. So I went for a drive. Beautiful afternoon. I was driving some back roads out near the river when I got the idea of stopping in at Golden Hills.

Esther: Where?

Lewis: Golden Hills.

Esther: You mean the Home for the Aged?

Lewis: Yeah, the retirement home up there on the hill overlooking the river.

Esther: What did you stop there for?

Lewis: To check around a little. They have a new West Wing, you know. Supposed to open any day now. Beautiful facility.

Esther: *(tone is very serious)* Lewis.

Lewis   Yeah?

Esther: You aren't going to, are you?

Lewis: I tried to reach Warren, but he wasn't home yet.

Esther: Lewis, please don't.

Lewis: What other choice do we have?

Esther: I don't know. *(pause)* What would he do there?

Lewis: What all the others do there.

Esther: Some of those places are awful.

Lewis: Some are. But the West Wing up there at Golden Hills is just like an apartment building. They have a new dining hall, a new chapel, a swimming pool—everything.

Esther: But he has a home.

Lewis: Does he?

Esther: I want him to.

Lewis: Do you think I don't want him to? As in business, for the good of everybody, there comes a time to make tough decisions. Esther, I need your help.

Esther: How?

Lewis: We must talk to Pop.

Esther: What if he won't go?

Lewis: Maybe there's another solution.

Esther: Maybe Warren and Beverly will take him. Is that why you called Warren?

Lewis: Are you kidding! No, we must talk to Pop. Maybe we can work it out. Maybe he really plans to marry Sally.

Esther: Warren would never stand for that. Denise would throw a long-distance fit!

Lewis: Don't get me started on Denise! My siblings don't want Pop to marry—but what are they going to say if we ask Pop to move out? Then we'll have several long-distance explosions!

Esther: Oh, Lewis, can't we just make it work?

Lewis: *(standing up to face her)* Esther, I want it to. I do want it to. But it's come to the place where I've decided that if it's a choice between you and Pop, then there is only one choice to be made. And the sooner, the better for everyone.

Esther: But I'm improving. Don't you think I'm better?

Lewis: *(nods)* And I want you to stay that way, honey. I want you to be happy and strong.

Esther: I want us all to be happy! *(She hugs him as though he were a refuge.)*

Charles: *(entering unnoticed downstage)* Hello.

Lewis: *(He and Esther pull apart in surprise as he turns toward Pop.)* Oh, Pop. I didn't hear you come in.

Charles: I'm sorry. I should ring the doorbell like everyone else, I guess.

Esther: You know better than that.

Lewis: Pop, Arnie said you had an accident. Are you okay?

Charles: I think I'm interrupting something.

Lewis: No, not really. Pop, are you feeling okay?

Esther: Was Sally hurt?

Charles: Look, it was no big deal. People got more excited than they needed to. Leland Miller just drove right into me. *(pause)* Look, I'll be heading back. I just wanted to hear more about these American International fellas.

Lewis: Well, like I told you at supper, I think we're making progress on a deal—

Charles: You don't need to go into it on my account. I just felt like talking, you know. That's all.

Lewis: Come and sit down, Pop. *(goes into the living room)* You too, Esther.

Charles: I really feel like I'm interrupting.

Lewis: Not at all. I was just coming over to see if you were okay, and Esther and I were saying we felt like there were certain things we oughta talk over. You can just lay that paper off the sofa, Pop. *(Charles move the paper as he sits on the right end of the sofa.)* Esther.

Esther: *(still standing near the kitchen table)* Maybe I should go out and fold some wash in the laundry.

Lewis: Come on. *(She comes across and sits in the armchair. Lewis watches, steps past her, and sits on the left end of the sofa. Charles watches them carefully.)* Now then. *(He smiles, trying to act calm.)* We had a few questions to ask you.

Charles: *(abruptly)* Shoot.

Lewis: Yes, well—ah, first of all—if it's not too personal—I guess we were really wondering how you feel about Sally.

Charles: I think you know.

Lewis: Not really, Pop. What I mean is, we were just asking ourselves if you might be planning marry her.

Charles: I know you're against it.

Lewis: I'm not. I know Esther's not.

Charles: *(looks at him sharply and stands)* What's going on here? *(Lewis doesn't reply.)* You two have been so upset about my seeing Sally. In fact, just this morning, Esther was saying—*(He catches himself, Lewis glances over at Esther who smiles at him as Charles sits down again.)* What are you getting at, Lewis?

Lewis: I just wanted to know if you plan to marry her?

Charles: *Marry* her? *(It seems a different idea to him.)* Well, when you put it that way—you mean if you children agreed?

Lewis: We don't have to approve what you do, Pop. You're on your own.

Charles: I am? Well, I don't know how to answer. Sally is a really swell woman.

Lewis: But you don't plan to marry her?

Charles: Hey, you're trying to trap me. *(stands up defensively)*

Lewis: No, we're not, Pop. We're just trying to plan for the future.

Charles: *(watching the two of them closely)* Oh, I get it. You're trying to marry me off.

Lewis: No, we're not.

Charles: First you try to take my license away—now you try to get rid of me by forcing me to marry Sally.

Lewis: *(laughing)* That's quite a switch! I never thought I'd hear you arguing *against* Sally.

Charles: You're cheating, Lewis. *(The doorbell rings.)*

Lewis: *(standing)* That must be Slick.

Charles: Oh, *he's* coming. The Gehman boy.

Lewis: Pop, we must talk about this soon. We're not happy living as we are—that's clear. We must find a solution.

Charles: *(looking unconvinced)* Why do I feel like you're the parent and I'm the child?

Lewis: I better get the door. *(goes downstage right)*

Charles: Well, I better go.

Esther: Why don't you stay, Pop?

Charles: Don't try to act nice now.

Esther: *(standing)* I mean it. Lewis would like it if you stayed. *(They look downstage right as Lewis enters with Slick*

Gehman, a wiry-looking salesman, dressed second-rate and chewing gum, his hair slicked back, wet against his scalp.)

Lewis: Yes, it certainly is. This is my wife, Esther, and my father, Charles Snavely. This is—let's see—

Slick: Gehman. Hello.

Lewis: Yes, I know—

Slick: Slick. How are you tonight? *(continues to chew as he pumps their hands, then spins to survey the room)*

Lewis: *(winces)* Yes, I wasn't sure if they always call you Slick or if maybe you use your regular first name—

Slick: Slick. *(chewing)* Slick's fine with me. Nice place, Lew. You mind if I chew?

Lewis: Pardon?

Slick: Gum.

Lewis: Oh. No.

Slick: No yes or no no.

Lewis: It's okay, I guess.

Slick: Thanks. *(He pulls out another big stick of chewing gum and puts it into his mouth.)*

Esther: I think I have some work to finish in the laundry if you'll excuse me, please. *(starts to cross toward the kitchen)*

Slick: *(chuckling)* Sure, don't let me keep you from your work. My mother—she's just like you—sorta frail looking— but work, work, work, work, —works her fingers to the bone—*(chuckles again, chewing)*

Esther: I see. Lucky woman. *(She looks at Lewis, smiling faintly as she retreats through the kitchen exit.)*

Lewis: Shall we sit at the kitchen table?

Slick: How old is this house, anyhow?

Lewis: Oh, about two hundred—give or take, right, Pop?

Slick: You born here?

Charles: Yes, I'd say about that. Let's see, the stone says 1766, so that would be more than two hundred years.

Slick: You born here?

Charles: *(not about to be pushed around by this yappy youngster)* My great-grandfather Lewis Snavely was the first one in our family born here, although *his* grandfather cut the trees down to start the farm. *(Slick waits for his question to be answered, pausing in his chewing to stare at Charles who doesn't miss a beat.)* Where were you born, Slick?

Slick: Huh? Oh, Upper Township. Never saw the place. My daddy says they tore it down to build a factory. Shoes. Storm windows of course?

Lewis: On the house?

Slick: And what kind of heat?

Lewis: Oil. And yes, we have storm windows.

Charles: Was your father a brother to Jack? The Gehman who sold tires over near Stoneridge Crossing?

Slick: Yeah, Jack's my daddy's brother all right. You know him?

Charles: Bought tires from him once. But I remember especially meeting him the day after Bernard Bucher's barn burned down—he was rooting around in those embers, everything still steaming—

Slick: Man, I could tell you some real stories about Uncle Jack and how he used that tire business to buy Sweeter's Restaurant.

Charles: He owns Sweeter's?

Slick: Yup.

Charles: I had no idea.

Slick: Most people don't. *(confidential)* I wouldn't want to say it's Mafia for sure, but you can bet on it.

Charles: Oh, go on!

Slick: Mafia's everywhere—what's your name again?

Charles: Charles.

Lewis: I guess I was interested in what you might have to say about the farm.

Slick: Sure, sure, Lew. Let me just say, Charlie, the Mafia's going to wipe out all of us, including you Snavely's, if we don't pay attention.

Charles: You're a little crazy. Your father know you talk like this?

Slick: *(insulted, looking from Charles to Lewis)* Is he in on selling this place?

Lewis: Well, not really, I guess—

Charles: Lewis and Esther own the farm. Elsa and I sold it to them eleven years ago.

Slick: Good. Well, let's get down to business. Mind if we sit at the table here?

Lewis: Go right ahead. *(Charles and Lewis exchange glances as Slick strides to the table, flips open his briefcase, and rolls out a sheaf of papers.)*

Slick: You don't look like much of a farmer, Lew. You really haul the manure and all that?

Lewis: We haven't had any livestock for several years. A neighbor helps me with most of the field work.

Slick: Did my daddy show you these?

Lewis: No, he didn't. *(He studies the papers; Charles stands at a safe distance, but it is obvious he is very interested.)*

Slick: Well, the party which is interested in buying your farm would like to develop it like this with apartment building: all along here—

Charles: Apartment buildings? *(moves closer)*

Slick: Yeah. *(He glances at Lewis as though to urge him to quiet his father.)* Of course this house could be developed much better than it is now into two plush apartments. *(Charles responds with a look of alarm.)*

Lewis: Looks like an awful lot of apartments on there. Are they the orange drawings?

Slick: Yeah.

Lewis: What are those green things?

Slick: Trees.

Charles: There aren't that many trees out there in those fields.

Slick: We'd plant them.

Charles: What about the farm?

Slick: What about it?

Charles: What would happen to the land?

Lewis: If we'd sell it, Pop, this wouldn't be a farm anymore. It would be a little village of apartment buildings and some nice shops.

Slick: You wouldn't even know the place, Charlie.

Lewis: How much—how much is your party offering?

Slick: Well, I didn't know if you wanted to discuss price here *(with a glance at Charles)* or if you should maybe look over these plans a little and then you could come to our office next week and we'll talk price.

Lewis: Can't you give me an idea?

Slick: Well, this is confidential material, of course. *(a glance at Charles)*

Lewis: It's okay. Pop lives with us.

Charles: Maybe I better leave you two alone—

Lewis: You stay here, Pop. Slick, what's the offer?

Slick: For the hundred and twenty-nine acres, including woods and everything, fourteen thousand per acre.

Charles: Fourteen thousand! Why, that's more than a million—

Slick: Almost two—

Charles: You hear that, Lewis?

Lewis: I hear it, Pop.

Charles: You going to take it?

Lewis: We'll have to talk it over. I'm not sure I want to sell the place.

Charles: I never lived anywhere else, you know. *(He recedes a bit in deference to his son.)*

Slick: My daddy says you're a rich man already.

Lewis: I doubt it.

Slick: He says he hears you're selling Horning and Snavely Equipment Company. Is that true?

Lewis: H & S isn't sold yet. Besides, I'm only a minority owner. Brian owns most of it.

Slick: Some people have the gravy—you'll be able to retire before you're fifty.

Lewis: I'll believe it when I see it.

Charles: Lewis'll never retire. He's too much of a Snavely.

Slick: Is that right? Here, Lew, let me show you what they'd do down here along the stream. They'd plan to build two footbridges and a regular street bridge.

Charles: Footbridges are a good idea down there. My father built one there when I was a boy, but it washed away in Hurricane Hazel. *(He sounds caught between sadness and anticipation.)*

Slick: Boy, my daddy say's that was some hurricane!

Lewis: I see. *(Clearly the visit is over for Lewis.)* Well, thanks for coming—

Charles: My mother's father, my Grandfather Yost, used to walk
           with a limp. And Mother always used to say it happened
           once in a blizzard years ago when Grandpa Yost was
           just a teenager. It was a savage blizzard, the way she
           told it, and they didn't have any snowplows or
           caterpillars in those days. It must have been more than
           two feet deep, the way she said, and everyone out in the
           country was stranded.

Slick: *(impatient but sort of polite)* Sounds like it was pretty
           rough in the old days, Charlie. Well, I better run along.

Charles: *(alternately walking, sitting, and standing as he talks)*
           Mother says my great-grandfather and his family could
           easily survive the storm because they had some cows and
           chickens and plenty of wood for the stove. But they
           worried about a poor family across the hill from them.
           The storm went on for several days and the temperatures
           were fierce and they were afraid this family might need
           help. I think she used to call them the Fultons. Anyhow,
           they asked Grandpa Yost, because he was the oldest and
           good with a horse, to take some food over to the Fultons
           and make sure they had some wood for their stove. So
           Grandpa went out into that blizzard, down across the
           frozen creek and over the hill to these Fulton people.
           Took him the better part of a morning, the way Mother
           said. And when he got there, he discovered they *had*
           plenty of food and plenty of wood. Grandpa left his sack
           of supplies there anyhow and then turned around and
           headed for home. But part way back to the farm he got
           caught in a terrible fury—that's what Mother always

called it, a "terrible fury"—and somehow his leg got caught between the horse and a pair of trees, throwing him off in this waist-high snow. Took him till early evening to get home, hanging on to that horse with his leg broken and that storm thrashing the trees along the creek. And of course it was impossible to go for a doctor. So they waited until the blizzard was over, and consequently Grandpa Yost always walked with a limp. *(Charles has told the story with tremendous fervor, his emotions rising in him as he relives the story, his voice almost breaking as he ends the story, his eyes full of tears Slick seems a little uncomfortable and Lewis simply watches and listens quietly—he is not indifferent but neither is he permitting Charles to make him feel guilty.)* You see, he went to help them, but no one could go to help him. *(There is a long awkward silence as Charles comes to his senses. He glances at Slick and Lewis, smiling faintly, looking at his watch, and giving the general impression of having momentarily lost his bearings.)* Oh, I'm sorry, I must have gotten carried away.

Lewis: That's okay, Pop.

Slick: Never heard that story before. That's a new one.

Charles: (still in a bit of a daze) Oh? Well, it's true. It really happened.

Slick: I'm sure. Well, I think I better shove off. Maybe we can get together next week. They'd like to start building as soon as possible.

Lewis: I told your dad I wasn't sure we'd sell. We'll need time to process your proposal. *(Phone rings, and Charles goes to answer.)*

Charles: Hello, Snavelys. Oh, Warren, Warren! How are you? Nice to hear your voice. Yes, he's here with a realtor. Say, how's Beverly and the children?

Bobby: *(entering downstage right)* Oh boy, what a dumb parade! I'm never going to the fair again.

M. Sue: *(right on his heels)* Good! You are such a pest.

Lewis: Children. *(They pause at his tone, staring at Slick.)*

Charles: *(laughing)* Oh, that's funny Warren. Okay, I'll let you speak to Lewis.

Lewis: This is Mr. Gehman from Timbers Realty. This is my son Bobby and my daughter, Margaret Sue. And that's my oldest son, Arnie. *(Arnie enters just as he is being introduced.)*

M. Sue: Hello.

Bobby: Hi. *(Arnie simply waves carelessly.)* I lost a dollar and Arnie wouldn't loan me any. I was so mad.

Esther: *(entering)* Bobby, you better come out here until you cool off.

Arnie: He's so sloppy with money. Can't see how he got elected.

Bobby: I am not.

Lewis: Boys. *(Margaret Sue has gone upstairs and Bobby follows his mother into the kitchen.)*

Charles: Warren's on the phone, Lewis.

Slick: Well, I'll be leaving, Lew. *(extends his hand)* Thanks for your time. I'll leave the drawings here, if that's okay.

Lewis: Sure. *(They shake.)*

Slick: *(extending his hand to Pop)* Nice meeting you, Charlie. Hang in there. *(They shake as Slick starts downstage right, nodding at Arnie.)* See you, son. *(Arnie watches him go out and then crosses to the table. Lewis goes to the phone.)*

Lewis: Hi, Warren. Thanks for calling back. Listen, will you be up for a while yet? *(pause)* Okay, I'll call you back within the hour. Bye.

Arnie: What's this?

Charles: They want to buy the farm.

Arnie: The farm? Our farm? You selling?

Lewis: I don't know. I kinda doubt it.

Charles: Where would you move?

Lewis: Hold it! We haven't made any decisions yet.

Arnie: When will we move, if we do?

Lewis: Didn't you hear what I said?

Arnie: Not before Thanksgiving, I hope.

Lewis: Arnie!

Arnie: I don't want that interrupting my football games.

Charles: *(abruptly, to Arnie)* Why don't you go downstairs and watch TV?

Arnie: *(taken aback)* What? You want me to go?

Charles: I want to talk to your father.

Arnie: Well, whatever you say, Grandpa. *(He seems slightly resentful and hums as he takes his time going to the kitchen door, disappears, re-enters, still humming, comes back to the table to take another look at the drawings, noisily chewing some chips he picked up in the kitchen, glances at the two of them, smiles, and goes back toward the kitchen door, pausing to turn, roll his eyes, and say in a singsongy tone)* Bye. I'm leaving now. But you never know when I'll be back. *(He exits, and immediately re-enters.)* Call me if you have an accident! *(He exits again.)*

Charles: *(after an awkward moment)* Lewis, I have one question. I know you're hoping to leave H & S so you have more time for Esther and the family.

Lewis: I promised Esther that the last time she went to Valley Vista.

Charles: I think that's commendable. But you've always been such a busy fellow, even when you were a teenager. What will you do?

Lewis: I'm not sure. I guess I'll try to go one step at a time. It struck me tonight that maybe instead of selling this place to Timber Realty, I could develop it myself. That way I'd be close to Esther.

Charles: I guess you want to sell the farm so you have something to live on. It's been in the family for seven generations, Lewis.

Lewis: I know. I'm not retiring, I'm just trying to find a way to reshape my life.

Charles: Look, son, we're grown-ups. If I'm becoming too much of a burden to you, you should just say so. I can move out—or get a housekeeper.

Lewis: Oh, I get it, Pop. You think we'd sell the farm to get rid of you.

Charles: I think I know when I'm not wanted.

Lewis: Oh, Pop! That's one of the main reasons I wouldn't sell.

Charles: In other words, one of the big things holding you back is not knowing what to do about me.

Lewis: I didn't say that.

Charles: You implied it.

Lewis: I meant it positive. You make it sound negative.

Charles: Why can't you just be honest with me?

Lewis: *(with exasperation)* I wish to God it were possible to be honest with everybody about everything every day of the year.

Charles: Try.

Lewis: *(chuckling with frustration)* It's so hard. Pop, I don't want Esther to have to leave me and the children again, it's that simple.

Charles: If you want me to go to a home, why don't you just say so?

Lewis: *(after a beat)* Maybe it's a good idea.

Charles: What!

Lewis: Maybe we should go have a look at several—and consider it.

Charles: Are you serious?

Lewis: You asked for honesty.

Charles: I bet you've already been to a bunch of them, haven't you, Lewis?

Lewis: Now, Pop, take it easy.

Charles: Answer me, haven't you?

Lewis: I think we better talk about this some other time. *(Margaret Sue comes down the steps, pausing to stare at them.)* Margaret Sue, you go on down to the family room with your brothers.

M. Sue: I'm sorry. I didn't know you two were arguing. *(starts toward the kitchen door)*

Lewis: We're not arguing.

M. Sue: *(spinning as she reaches the door)* "Discussing." *(She disappears.)*

Lewis: Pop, I want so badly for things to work out. For all of us.

Charles: I do, too. I really do.

Lewis: I know. If only you and Esther could get along.

Charles: *(nods)* I think I better go. *(He goes to leave; the phone rings; Lewis goes to answer as Charles watches.)*

Lewis: Hello. Hi, Brian. *(listens, then voice intensifies)* What! Are they crazy! No way. You hear me, Brian—no way. Why didn't Joe tell them that? *(pause)* And what did they say? *(pause)* Oh, that's just great. Listen, Joe gotta get to their lawyer tonight and tell them—no way am I staying on. You got it, Brian—or shall I call Joe myself! *(pause)* Okay, let me know what he says. Right. See ya. *(He hangs up, stands by the phone a moment, sighs, turns to Charles.)* That Joe Moorefield can really be dumb sometimes. Put him and Brian together and you get a real stupid mishmash. *(walks towards Pop)* That American International lawyer's trying to blackmail me into staying on after they buy H & S. Brian's going to retire in Florida, he says. That's okay. But they're acting like they'll blow the deal if I don't stay and help run things.

Charles: Doesn't sound like they want Brian to stay on!

Lewis: *(chuckling)* These New York guys aren't as dumb as they act. They can spot a hot air balloon as well as the next guy. I think I better call Joe myself to make sure he gets the message.

Charles: So what's going to happen?

Lewis: Look, it's not my problem. I have decided to simplify my life. When Esther and I were farming—even when we had dairy—we were happy. She was as strong as I've ever seen her. Oh, sure, we were tied down, but we were together. Now we're tied down separately. But that's going to change. I told Brian I was quitting last spring. You should have seen his face! So he decided to sell and I said I'd stay until he got it sold—but no longer than six months. It's now *seven* months.

Charles: Couldn't you work for these New York guys? If they want you so bad, wouldn't they give you shorter hours! A man has to have a job.

Lewis: You know me better than that, Pop. I'd go crazy seeing other people run H & S into the ground. Listen, I made a decision and I plan to stick by it. Esther and I must be together more—and I must live with less stress in my job. It just flows on to her.

Charles: Well, I better be heading back to my side.

Lewis: You okay, Pop?

Charles: *(nods)* Yeah. I'm sorry about everything, Lewis. If only your mother hadn't died.

Lewis: *(putting his hand on his father's shoulder affectionately)* We have to accept our situation and try to cope. You know, I'd be willing to have a little less money and a little more happiness in this house.

Charles: I believe you. Good night, Lewis.

Lewis: Good night, Pop. Sleep well.

Charles: I hope I didn't upset things too much.

Lewis: No.

Charles: Sorry about the accident at the fair. *(suddenly, pensively)* Sometimes I feel lost. Like my mind swims away from me for a few moments. And then it's back. But you never know when it's going to happen. *(looks at his son)* It's sorta scary, Lewis. I remember Grandpap and the way he got.

Lewis: Now, now, Pop. It's not that bad. You don't worry about it.

Charles: *(nods reluctantly)* Good night. *(He goes out. Lewis watches after him, then goes back to the table and starts gathering up the drawings as Esther enters from the kitchen.)*

Esther: Margaret Sue says you were arguing.

Lewis: *(looks at her, his tone weary)* His mind is slipping more all the time, honey. It sort of frightens me. He seems so normal until all of a sudden he loses his bearings, and I find myself starting to treat him like a child. He called it swimming. "Sometimes my mind swims away from me," he said.

Esther: I know the feeling.

Lewis: *(looking at her sharply)* Hey, none of that.

Esther: But I do. I suppose that's why I don't want you to make him leave. He can't help it.

Lewis: Hey, I'm open to any solution. God knows, I only want peace in this house.

Esther: I know, Lewis. But I don't want you to send him away. *(Lewis looks at her, raises his hands in a shrug, drawings in hand, heaves a big sigh, and turns and carries the drawings to the desk. Esther looks after him, then turns downstage, eyes worried, and sighs herself. Lights down as scene ends.)*

(CURTAIN)

Act Two, *Scene One*

(Two months have passed. We see the same set, only there have been numerous additions of antiques. The house was nicely arranged with a touch of class in Act One; now there seems to be a mix of the old and the new, including an antique light hanging over the kitchen table. Esther has a few Thanksgiving decorations mixed in.

Charles is alone, studying the new Dutch cupboard in the dining room. It is the evening after Thanksgiving in November. Dinner's over and the light is fading. Arnie comes running down the stairs two at a time. He is dressed to jog on a cool fall evening. He notices Charles.)

Arnie: Oh, you're still here, Grandpa?

Charles: Yes, I was just studying this new cupboard Lewis bought. He sure is buying some snazzy antiques.

Arnie: I think it's really neat that he and Mom can do that together.

Charles: Yes, it is.

Arnie: Where's Uncle Warren?

Charles: Oh, he went over to my side. I guess he'll be sleeping over there with me tonight. I'll be shoving off myself now.

Arnie: I didn't mean you needed to. I just didn't realize you were still here after supper. But it's certainly okay.

Charles: Yeah, well, Warren and I got talking to Lewis and Esther before they left to take Bobby and Margaret Sue to their activities at church. You going for a run?

Arnie: Gotta stay in shape.

Charles: You worried about the game next week with the Bears?

Arnie: I don't have time to think about that. I'm concentrating on the Centerville game tomorrow afternoon.

Charles: It's good you concentrate, Arnie. You're a good player. You never get nervous or worried?

Arnie: Oh, I guess everyone does sometimes.

Charles: You gotta believe in yourself, Arnie. Even when the going gets rough, believe in yourself. Think positive. Concentrate!

Arnie: Thanks, Grandpa. I really appreciate your support. *(goes to leave, hesitates, then turns)* You worried about tomorrow, Grandpa?

Charles: What? This table's sticky again.

Arnie: You worried about moving tomorrow?

Charles: *(offhand)* It's just another day.

Arnie: You gotta believe in yourself too, Grandpa.

Charles: *(a little too quickly)* Oh, I do. I do, Arnie.

Arnie: Must be hard to leave a place where you've lived all your life.

Charles: Yes, it'll be a change. But I'll survive, I'm sure.

Warren: *(entering)* Pop, I found this—*(notices Arnie)* Oh hi, Arnie. You off for a little jogging?

Arnie: Yeah, I guess. I'll see you later, Uncle Warren. *(He goes out. Warren is about forty, more stocky than Lewis, dressed in coat and tie.)*

Charles: I'm sorry, I was just looking at this new Dutch cupboard Lewis bought.

Warren: I went for this article about our school system which caused such a fuss when the newspaper printed it.

Charles: You like antiques, Warren?

Warren: Beverly does. You want to see this article?

Charles: *(reaching for the news clipping)* How are Beverly and the children, Warren? *(starts to read clipping)*

Warren: Fine. *(looks at the Dutch cupboard more closely himself)* As fine as one can be in Fort Wayne at this time of the year. Sorry I couldn't bring them along. But when we got Esther's letter I just felt I should get in here as fast as possible to talk some sense into my brother's head.

Charles: Tell them I said hello. It's nice that at least you could be here for Thanksgiving.

Warren: Sure, Pop. Beverly's awful busy these days working on several social benefits—you know, for the Cancer Society and stuff. I hardly get to see her half the time, what with my school meetings several nights a week.

Charles: You going to be a principal all your life?

Warren: *(He has been moving around, looking at things throughout both rooms while this scene is happening; now he stops, looks at Pop, and chuckles uncomfortably.)* Well, Pop, I don't know. Being principal's not a very easy job, even though it's junior high. People don't appreciate you, the way I see it.

Charles: Sounds like teaching.

Warren: Oh, that's right, you did substitute teaching for a few years.

Charles: Yeah. Squeezed it in before I went full-time at H & S. Always liked teaching.

Warren: Well, in teaching you can get response. Some students may like you and some not. But the point is some do. You have an arena in which to prove yourself. But being principal is different. No one likes a principal.

Charles: Teachers do.

Warren: Not in Fort Wayne. *(pause)* You think I should quit?

Charles: Warren, you know I've always said you should either like what you do or like what you do.

Warren: You mean, do what you like.

Charles: What?

Warren: *(raises his voice a bit, as though his father is hard of hearing, which he isn't)* I think you meant to say like what you do or do what you like.

Charles: That's what I said.

Warren: Sure, Pop. I probably wasn't listening. *(pause)* How do you feel about tomorrow?

Charles: Warren, if you came here to stir things up, I think you'll probably end up doing more harm than good.

Warren: You didn't answer my question.

Charles: *(gets up from the table)* One must be realistic, Warren.

Warren: Have you been to Golden Hills yet?

Charles: We were up twice. First time Lewis took me and the second time both he and Esther were along.

Warren: Well?

Charles: The main building is enough to make you croak. I think they're going to renovate it. But the West Wing is beautiful. More than adequate.

Warren: You're really planning on going, aren't you? *(Charles doesn't answer Warren but looks at him instead.)* Why?

Charles: Not since the first morning outside the garden of Eden has there been an answer to that question.

Warren: I beg your pardon.

Charles: Anyone who asks an old man "why" has to be a little crazy.

Warren: I'm sorry, Pop, I didn't mean anything by it.

Charles: It's okay.

Warren: Are you upset?

Charles: *(half angry)* Wouldn't you be? *(looking out into the audience as though out the window)* I remember as though it were yesterday that cold winter night when we were sledding up there on the hill, and the others had wandered back to the house here for some hot chocolate, and I pulled the deacon's daughter down beside me on a fallen tree and asked her to marry me. She was five years younger than me, you know. Cream of the crop! Beautiful Elsa, full moon, and a timid Snavely boy. "Yes," she said, "I'd love it!" *(His voice is bright.)* That's what she said, sitting there on that log in the snow, her pretty eyes bright as the stars. "I'd love it!" *(His voice has risen with emotion, his eyes filling with tears; now his voice falls to almost a whisper.)* And now she's gone. Gone from the earth. Gone from the home place. And me, too.

Warren: *(coming downstage to stand behind his father)* Pop, we must stop Lewis.

Charles: It's too late. Besides, Lewis contacted you and Denise about it, didn't he? I know he wrote to Marian in Jordan. She sent me a nice letter.

Warren: Yes, he did phone me. But I'm not going to let him get away with it. You're coming to Fort Wayne with me.

Charles: What?

Warren: You're coming to Fort Wayne with me, Pop. Tomorrow.

Charles: *(astonished)* To live?

Warren: Of course, to live. Come over here and sit down. We'll call Beverly and tell her.

Charles: Where? Where would I stay? I've never been to your new place, but from your descriptions I've always thought it was pretty small for two growing children.

Warren: Pop, I'm sorry I never offered it before. We'll work it out somehow. Our house is probably not quite as small as we left on.

Charles: Really. Where would I stay?

Warren: We could build an addition.

Charles: Warren, now stop and think before you do anything rash.

Warren: We could at least develop a room for you in the basement.

Charles: Maybe I don't want to live out there in the boonies.

Warren: The boonies? Fort Wayne? Oh, Pop, you'd love Indiana.

Charles: Would I? Well, let me ask you this. What would you do if I needed care?

Warren: We'd look after you.

Charles: No, if I really deteriorated and someone needed to watch me the way we spent years caring for Grandpap and Grandmom right here in this house? Would you *or* Beverly take care of me?

Warren: We both would.

Charles: Why don't you call her and ask her.

Warren: *(going to phone)* Okay, I will.

Charles: Warren, thanks for the offer. I appreciate it, I really do.

Warren: I'm dialing. *(dials)*

Charles: Warren, think it through before you act in haste.

Warren: It's ringing.

Charles: Ask her if she's willing to spend five or ten years of her life taking care of a decrepit old man who becomes more nauseating every day.

Warren: Pop, that's an awful way to talk—hello, Beverly—oh Ashley, it's you. This is Daddy. How are you this evening? Good. Where? Well, whatever your mother says. No, Ashley, you listen on her, you hear me? Okay.

Is Mother there? May I talk to her? Sure. *(to Charles)*
She has some women over for a planning session.

Charles: How old is Ashley now?

Warren: She's fourteen—and becoming quite the lady.
Beverly—how are you this evening? What? No, I just
wanted to say hello and let you know everything's going
fine on this end—no, nothing's wrong—Uh-huh—sure,
Beverly, I understand. Listen, I want to ask you a questio
What? When? Oh, I'm sure that'll be just fine. Sure,
I'll take care of the children. Listen, about this
question—really? You mean for the National Society?
Congratulations. When's the election? *(long pause)*
Well, that's good news. What? No, I don't think so.
Okay, Beverly. Sure, I understand. Tell Junior I said
hello. Bye now. *(Warren hangs up slowly, and without
glancing at Charles, slams down the phone. He is angry.
He takes off his jacket, tosses it across a chair, and paces
back and forth, banging his fist on the table each time he
comes near.)*

Charles: *(disappointed)* It's okay, Warren, I appreciate the
consideration.

Warren: Oh, I'm so sorry. Beverly just—she doesn't understand
these things. *(His tone is very emotional.)* Boy, she's
gonna hear about this!

Charles: But you didn't even ask her.

Warren: I didn't need to. *(stops)* I don't like the way you said
that, Pop. Maybe Beverly's not the ideal wife, but you
don't have to imply anything.

Charles: I didn't mean to.

Warren: She's several stripes better than Esther, I'll tell you that. *(They are standing apart now, anger in the room about them.)*

Charles: I won't have you criticizing Esther, Warren.

Warren: I didn't mean to. *(pause)* Oh, Pop what are we going to do?

Charles: Golden Hills won't be that bad.

Warren: But it's not home. You belong here, Pop. This is where you were born. You farmed this land. Snavelys don't go to old people's homes. They take care of their own, just like you took care of your parents and Grandpap took care of his.

Charles: A lot of people like these retirement villages.

Warren: You won't. Penned away from the rest of society, waiting to die. I've seem them in Fort Wayne. You belong here, Pop. It's the only place you'll really be happy.

Charles: I have to agree with you there. *(He hears a car driving in and walks downstage right, peering out.)* It sounds like Lewis and Esther just drove in, Warren. Now I don't want you arguing with him, you hear? He's had it awfully rough this past month, trying to phase out at H & S, and trying to figure out what to do next.

Warren: He's selling the home place and kicking you out, and you pity him, Pop!

Charles: Warren, you know you've been a special son over the years. But Lewis is special, too. I know you two have had your troubles, but I don't want to be mixed up in that. You treat him right, you hear? *(Warren looks at him but does not nod.)*

Lewis: *(as he and Esther enter)* Back again. You two behaving?

Charles: *(laughing)* Yeah, we didn't get over to my side yet. We got to talking.

Warren: Where are the kids?

Esther: They're still at church. Lewis, I think I'll head off to bed, if that's okay.

Lewis: Already?

Esther: Yes, I need my rest.

Lewis: Fine. I'll go get the kids after a while. Sleep well. I'll be up later on. I have to finish that report for Brian tonight yet.

Esther: Good night, Pop. Warren.

Charles: Good night, Esther. Sleep well.

Warren: Good night, Esther.

Esther: I'll make breakfast for everyone in the morning. You like squirting grapefruit, Warren?

Warren: *(laughs)* Sure. And thanks again for dinner. *(Esther nods and disappears.)*

Charles: She has a knack for buying grapefruit that can squirt you in the eye everytime!

Lewis: *(explaining)* We went to see Dr. Elder after we dropped the kids off and he wants her to get more rest.

Warren: What does the doctor say? Won't she ever get over it?

Lewis: *(touchy)* Get over what?

Warren: Won't she ever be—well, I shouldn't have been so nosey, I guess.

Lewis: Esther needs more rest, less stress, and a husband who's more available.

Warren: I see. Well, I'm glad she's doing better.

Charles: You ready to hit the hay, Warren?

Warren: Pop, I was hoping we could talk to Lewis before we head to bed.

Charles: Are you sure?

Warren: Do you mind, Lewis? May we talk to you a bit?

Lewis: Talk.

Warren: Maybe we ought to sit down.

Lewis: Help yourself. I'm sorta tired of sitting myself. And thirsty. You want a soft drink?

Warren: Pop?

Charles: No thanks. *(He walks over and sits in the armchair in the living room, sidestepping the confrontation between the brothers.)*

Lewis: How about you, Warren?

Warren: You have 7-Up?

Lewis: I'll check. *(He goes into the kitchen and Warren and Pop look at each other, Warren anticipating, Pop reluctant. Warren is pacing as Lewis re-emerges.)* Here we go. The last one, Warren. I'll split it with you.

Warren: Thanks.

Lewis: *(testing his brother)* So how's principaling?

Warren: Okay. How's antiquing?

Lewis: *(looking at him with a smile equal to the quarrel)* Fine.
         I just came up with a new idea today.

Charles: What's that, Lewis?

Lewis: Well, I've been thinking about what to do with your end
         of the house. We could rent it. But it struck me that if
         we're really going to get into antiques—and if I hold
         on to the farm and keep farming the good land and break
         up the 20 acres of woods into development of beautiful
         homes—then it would make a lot of sense to have our
         office here at home.

Warren: *(chagrined)* What?! *(Charles is startled too.)*

Lewis: Well, maybe now's not the appropriate time to say it, but
         it's just an idea. That way I could be closer to Esther
         and the kids. Assuming, of course, that the deal with
         H & S goes through. We ran into another snag today on
         one of the clauses in the contract.

Warren: Hold it, hold it, hold it! *(loud)* You mean to tell me,
         Lewis, that you're going to convert what we've always
         called the "grandparents house" into an office for *selling
         antiques and land?* You must have lost your senses.
         What about Pop?

Lewis: Pop's going to Golden Hills, aren't you, Pop? *(Charles
         doesn't answer.)*

Warren: *(angry)* Boy, you sure got the gall. Not only do you let
         Pop have the short end of the stick on both ends, but

you're trying to nail the last spike into his coffin if you can. You seem to like old things, but you sure don't like old people!

Lewis: *(shouting)* Oh, shut up, Warren. You don't have the slightest idea what this is all about!

Warren: Oh, I don't, huh? It doesn't take a brilliant mind to see when someone's being shafted, Lewis. And that man right there is being shafted. By you! He spent the better part of a decade of his life taking care of his senile father and his bedfast mother.

Lewis: Where do you think I was when that was going on?

Warren: So what happens when he gets older and his wife dies? He gets sent away to one of these homes where people stand in line, waiting to get on the conveyor belt which goes over the brink—only you never know how far you are from the end once you're on. Man, you have some nerve!

Lewis: I have nerve, do I? What's holding you back, Warren?

Warren: What?

Lewis: What's keeping you from packing up Pop and taking him to Indiana with you?

Warren: I offered.

Lewis: *(laughing angrily)* Oh, wow, that's great! And why aren't you packing?

Warren: Because it wouldn't work.

Lewis: There's one in every family!

Warren; Don't you point a finger at me, brother!

Lewis: Why don't you try to stand in my shoes for one moment, Warren?

Warren: *He* did! And he stood up like a man and took care of his parents when they were old! *He* did!

Charles: *(standing up, his voice anguished)* Boys! Oh, boys, boys, boys. I won't have you talking to each other this way. *(exhausted)* Sit down and keep your mouths shut. *(All three sit down and fall into silence.)*

Warren: *(after a bit)* I'm sorry, Pop. I meant it all for your good.

Charles: I know. But I think it's better if we don't discuss it anymore. Enough's been said. Too much, in fact. *(Arnie enters downstage right, on the trot, punching his fists as he prances through the room, obviously having run several miles.)* Hello, Arnie.

Arnie: *(constantly in motion)* Hi, Grandpa. Dad. Uncle Warren. *(He prances toward the kitchen.)* Don't worry, I just want a drink. I'll be out of your way in a jiffy. *(He prances into the kitchen, re-entering carrying a glass of orange juice, prances around Lewis and Warren, punching playfully, then starts up the stairs, turning in his motion with a sweep of his hand.)* Carry on, carry on. I'm out of sight! *(He exits up the stairs.)*

Charles: He's a good football player, you know.

Warren: So I hear.

Charles: I wouldn't be a bit surprised he makes All County, if not this year, at least next season in his senior year.

Warren: *(to Lewis)* You must be proud of him.

Lewis: He's a good boy.

Charles: *(after a slight pause)* Say, did I ever tell you about the time Grandpa Yost got caught in a snow blizzard?

Lewis: Yes, I've heard it, Pop. But maybe Warren hasn't.

Warren: Yes, several times. But I'd be glad to hear it again.

Charles: *(laughing self-consciously)* I guess I'm so old I tell things over again and again.

Lewis: That's okay, Pop, don't worry about it.

Charles: Old Mike Hollinger's dead, you know, Warren.

Warren: No, I didn't.

Charles: Suicide.

Warren: Really?

Charles: Yeah, he and his wife have been at the Northwest Nursing Home for several years now. She's really bad off, the way I hear. Can't talk and can't eat by herself. I guess it just got to Mike.

Warren: Was he sick?

Charles: Not that I know of.

Warren: How? *(Pop doesn't seem to want to answer, so Warren glances at Lewis.)*

Lewis: *(quietly)* He went down to that pond at the lower end of the property and just walked in.

Warren: That's awful.

Charles: Funny how he could have lived and she should have died.

Warren: Yeah, life's strange sometimes.

Charles: Well, I think I better be getting to bed so I can get up in the morning. *(He gets up.)* Good night, Lewis.

Warren: I guess I'll walk over with you now, Pop. Might as well experience as much of that place as I can before it becomes a plush office. *(Lewis glances at him but refuses to fight.)*

Lewis: Good night, Pop. Sleep well.

Charles: Thanks, Lewis. You know, Warren, Old Mike left a note. "God gave us a brain," it said, "and that includes deciding when to die." Or something like that.

Lewis: *(talking suddenly to this father as he would to his son)* Pop. I think you better put Mike out of your mind.

Charles: Don't worry, I'd never do that. It just makes a person wonder when someone like Mike does it.

Lewis: *(firm)* You heard what I said.

Charles: I hear you. Well, let's go, Warren, if we're going.

Warren: Okay. *(to Lewis)* See you in the morning.

Lewis: *(nods)* Good night. *(They go out, Lewis watching them, then twisting a soft drink can in frustration. Arnie appears on the steps, calm, and concerned.)*

Arnie: *(quietly—the real Arnie relating to the real Lewis)* They gone?

Lewis: Yeah.

Arnie: Thank God, it's almost over.

Lewis: *(sadly)* It's never going to be over, Arnie, as long as we live. We won't even fully understand it when we ourselves are dying. *(Slight pause as they seem locked in their thoughts.)*

(CURTAIN)

Act Two, *Scene Two*

(It is late evening, the same day. Lewis is walking around, straightening up the rooms and snapping lights when the telephone rings. He goes to answer.)

Lewis: Hello. *(pause)* Denise! Is that you? Hey, how you doing? Really? When? For four months? Well, I'll tell Pop about it. And Warren. He's here visiting. What? Oh, I think he's holding up okay. Yes, we're going ahead with our plans. *(listens)* What can I say more than I said during our last phone call? If you or Warren care to host Pop, that's fine with me. No, I'm not implying that. I'm not implying anything. *(Warren enters, dressed in his bathrobe.)* Yes, of course. Well, I can see that it would be hard. No, he doesn't say much, but I know it's on his mind. Okay, Denise, well thanks for calling. *(pause)* What? No, there aren't any plans for a sale. He's stored a good many things here and he's taking a lot along. What did you have in mind? The clock? *(noncommittal)* Okay, I'll keep that in mind if Pop decides to sell it or to give it to one of the children. What was that? *(can't believe his ears)* Mom's Bible? *(pause)* Denise, I'm trying to be fair with you—why do you say that? *(listens)* I have nothing to say, sister. I've tried the best I've known how. What? Well, I'm sorry. I really am. You want to talk to Warren—he just walked in. Denise? Denise? *(He slowly hangs up.)* She hung up on me! Little punk. Boy, was she in a bad mood.

Warren: Oh well, Lewis, that's Denise. Was she trying to buy something?

Lewis: I don't know. She heard Esther and I are getting into antiques, she said, and she hopes she has a chance for some of Pop's and Mom's things. Whatever that means. Looks like I'm not the only one who likes old things better than old people.

Warren: Lewis, I shouldn't have said that. I came back here to apologize. I know you and Esther have done so much for Mom and Pop. I'm sorry we had an argument.

Lewis: It's okay. I realize it's a very emotional time.

Warren: She mentioned Mom's Bible?

Lewis: Yeah, can you imagine that? She hasn't been to church in ten years and wants Mom's Bible.

Warren: She sounds as confused as the rest of us. *(walks to window, looking out at the night)* I must admit, I have so many feelings I can't express, Lewis. Like how I feel about this place. I wish I had the money to buy it from you if you're going to sell it, so it wouldn't leave the family.

Lewis: Would Pop stay here then?

Warren: Oh, I'm sure we'd find a way to work it out. He was born here, you know. So was I.

Lewis: Where does it say that you have to live where you were born? You sure don't now, Warren.

Warren: I miss it though. Remember how Hiram's cows used to get out and come over here in our cornfields? *(laughs)* Is that guy still living?

Lewis: Yeah, I'm afraid so. And his cows still break down his fences. We buy our milk from him, now that we don't have dairy anymore. Pop enjoys *(pause)*—enjoyed— walking over there for it every day, except in the winter.

Warren: No more of that, I guess.

Lewis: *(smiling)* Warren, you remember when we had some of our cousins here overnight—Fred and Benny and Sam— and several others. And we decided to put the farm wagon up on the barn roof?

Warren: *(laughing)* Yeah, I remember that!

Lewis: I can still see Pop's face when he came out of the house that morning and saw the wagon on the barn roof. Boy, did he let out a holler!

Warren: *(laughing)* Yeah. Reminds me of the time we threw Benny in the creek. Can't remember what prank he'd pulled on us, but I sure remember how funny he looked!

Lewis: Yeah, I remember that!

Warren: Whatever happened to Benny?

Lewis: He's a missionary in Africa.

Warren: Could have guessed. Funny how the wild ones always become preachers or missionaries.

Lewis: You're right about that, Warren.

Warren: Well, I'll be heading back to bed, Lewis. Just didn't feel right about our argument and wanted to make sure we're not mad at each other for life.

Lewis: I appreciate your coming over.

Warren: *(goes to leave, then pauses)* Mind if I ask you a question, Lewis?

Lewis: Of course not.

Warren: What do you want to do with the rest of your life?

Lewis: I want to be with my family. I've done well in farming and in business. Now it's time to concentrate on family. And I want Esther to be the happy and strong woman I married.

Warren: Are you really leaving H & S just because of Esther?

Lewis: I don't understand.

Warren: *(coming back several steps)* Is she that sick?

Lewis: No, she's not—well, I don't know how to answer you, Warren.

Warren: I admit it's none of my business. Part of it is wanting to know because I care about you folks, I guess. And another part of it is that I keep trying to understand why Pop has to leave here when he can take care of himself and he has his own set-up right here next to you folks. Esther seems to be the only answer.

Lewis: Isn't that good enough?

Warren: I guess. It's just that—

Lewis: Is Beverly willing?

Warren: Well, maybe if we found—well—probably not.

Lewis: So why does that make Esther such a villain?

Warren: I don't mean to imply anything of the like. I'm just trying to understand her. I never have.

Lewis: She's sensitive. She can be so strong, so self-assured.

Warren: How do you understand it? Or don't you?

Lewis: Oh, I understand my wife as well as I understand myself.

Warren: And?

Lewis: Warren, I don't think there's anything else I can tell you.

Warren: You mean there isn't anything else you're willing to tell me.

Lewis: You just automatically think the worst of me, don't you?

Warren: No, Lewis, I don't. I've always envied you two. But it's like you're protecting some secret about Esther.

Lewis: Well, well. Secrets and envy in the same breath.

Warren: Am I right? *(Lewis looks hard at Warren, paces, then comes back to Warren, looking straight at him.)*

Lewis: *(tersely)* Her father had an affair.

Warren: What?

Lewis: Can I trust you, Warren?

Warren: Sure.

Lewis: I've never told this to anyone. Esther, to my knowledge, has told only Dr. Elder and our pastor.

Warren: I understand. You can trust me.

Lewis: Pop must never, never know.

Warren: You have my word.

Lewis: *(pacing, then confidentially)* When Esther was a teenager, just out of high school, she saw her father with a young woman. Kissing. She followed them to a motel.

But Esther's dad never saw her, never knew that she knew. And she's never told him.

Warren: I can't believe it. Her dad, Elmer, had an affair? Does her mother know?

Lewis: We can't be sure. Esther thinks she doesn't. She could never bring herself to confront her dad. And she definitely doesn't want her mother to find out about it.

Warren: Are they still involved in church?

Lewis: Sure. Since when have church people become perfect?

Warren: So Esther has this all bottled up inside herself?

Lewis: You must remember, Warren, how much time she spent taking care of our mother when she was dying. Esther wasn't even a daughter—she's an in-law. And Charlie's grouchy, we all know that—he'll become more and more cantankerous. How can she stomach that—and keep remembering her own father with that young woman?

Warren: In other words, she doesn't trust men?

Lewis: That's a little overdrawn.

Warren: And with you gone so much—

Lewis: That was a factor. I've never fooled around, but when I was away so much, her imagination—

Warren: I understand. *(pause)* Well, that sure helps me to understand better. It's like our father reminds her of her father.

Lewis: I guess.

Warren: Sad thing is that our father has to pay the price for her dad's transgression.

Lewis: That's totally unfair, Warren.

Warren: I'm just trying to understand, Lewis.

Lewis: *(irritated)* You have a funny way of trying to understand. You go around making all these accusations, and then you try to act surprised when people are hurt.

Warren: Lewis, that's absolutely unfair.

Lewis: Absolutely!? I knew I shouldn't have told you. Why don't we start discussing Beverly and her family!

Warren: Oh, come on, Lewis. You get so carried away. Why don't we just drop it.

Lewis: *(warning)* Not a word to anyone.

Warren: I gave my word. Look, I better head on back to Pop's side.

Lewis: If I ever hear that you told Pop—

Warren: Lewis, I promise! I came over here to make peace, but it sounds like anything but peace.

Lewis: Maybe it's time we both went to bed.

Warren: *(turns abruptly and heads for the door, pausing before exit)* Good night, Lewis. *(Warren goes out, Lewis looks after him, then slowly snaps out the three remaining lights and heads upstairs in the dark.)*

(CURTAIN)

Act Two, *Scene Three*

(The next morning. Esther's clearing the table. Arnie comes down the stairs, dressed for jogging.)

Esther: Where do you think you're going, Arnie?

Arnie: I'm going for a run.

Esther: We're just about to leave.

Arnie: I'm not going along.

Esther: Yes, you are.

Arnie: Hey, I have this big game this afternoon, Mom. I can't possibly spend all morning going up to that Golden Hills place.

Esther: Arnie, I insist. Shall I call your father?

Lewis: *(coming down the stairs)* What's the problem, Arnie?

Esther: He doesn't want to go along.

Arnie: I gotta get ready for the game with Centerville.

Lewis: *(firm)* I'd like you to go, Arnie. We want to all go along as a family.

Arnie: Great!

Lewis: Would you please check the gas in the station wagon?

Arnie: Oh, all right. But I'm not happy about it.

Lewis: It's a hard morning for all of us, Arnie. *(Arnie exits. Lewis goes to check something at the desk, then turns to Esther.)* Today Pop goes home.

Esther: It's not a home, Lewis. They call it a home, but it's not a home.

Lewis: It will be. Hundreds of people live there and call it home.

Esther: I hate homes—retirement homes, rest homes, homes for children, homes for this, homes for that.

Lewis: Easy, Esther. It's almost over.

Esther: No, it's not. And you know that, Lewis. Don't you feel one bit guilty for what you're doing? And on Thanksgiving weekend, of all times.

Lewis: Golden Hills sets the schedule. *(pause)* Esther, we're in this together. It isn't fair for you to act that way.

Esther: Are *you* going to argue with me after Pop's gone?

Lewis: You know, I remember hearing Herbert Miller say years ago that while a man may think it's heroic to take care of his aging parents, even at the expense of his own family, it may in fact be a sign of weakness if a man can't say "no" to his parents. Sometimes I wonder why Pop refused to make some of his brothers and sisters help take care of Grandmom and Grandpap during those long years.

Esther: I still wish it wouldn't have to happen this way. I believe I hear Pop on the porch. I hope he didn't hear us talking. *(Lewis glances at her but says nothing; he does feel like he said more than he intended to. Charles enters downstage right.)*

Charles: Where is everybody?

Lewis: Oh, I'm not sure. I thought Warren went over with you after breakfast.

Charles: Yes, he's packing the last box for me.

Lewis: And Arnie's filling the station wagon with gas, Margaret Sue's upstairs studying, and Bobby's down watching TV. I'll call them if you're ready.

Charles: I'm ready whenever you are, Lewis.

Esther: *(suddenly)* Are you scared, Pop?

Charles: *(a bit surprised)* Scared? Why, yes, to be truthful, I am a bit scared. I've always lived here. I was born here, I raised my family here, and I've watched you raise yours here. I've never lived anywhere else. But now I'm moving to a new place and that's a little frightening. New faces, new sounds and smells, new surroundings.

Esther: Pop, you know we never meant it to work out this way.

Charles: I know.

Lewis: Pop, you know we're behind you. *(with intense affection)* I have no doubt that you'll make the journey safely.

Charles: I guess he was scared too, don't you think?

Lewis: Who?

Charles: Jesus.

Lewis: Jesus?

Charles: Yeah, Warren was just helping me to pack that picture of Jesus in the garden. Elsa gave it to me for my

birthday years ago. I suddenly realized he must have
been scared to die, too.

Lewis: I guess he was different, Pop.

Charles: It must have been terrible. The Bible says he *shouted,*
Lewis. *(voice raised)* "Why have you forsaken me?"
Shouted. Like he was scared. On that lonely hill.

Lewis: I know you've got the guts, Pop. Do you have the
courage?

Charles: *(nodding, more in control now)* God has promised us
that much, Lewis. Courage. *(pause)* Well, maybe we
better be going.

Warren: *(entering, sensing he's invading something)*
Everything's all packed.

Lewis: I better call the children.

Arnie: *(entering)* Car's ready.

Lewis: *(calling)* Bobby, we're ready to go. *(upstairs)*
Margaret Sue, come on down if you're going along.

Esther: *(crossing to Pop)* Pop, why don't you just stay?

Charles: Now, Esther.

Esther: *(taking his hand imploringly)* I'm feeling much better
this morning and I really believe we can work it out.
*(Everyone watches, Margaret Sue pausing on the steps
as she enters. Everyone but Charles looks at Lewis.
Bobby enters, unaware of the atmosphere.)*

Bobby: What's happening?

Warren: *(after a pause)* Lewis, I don't know how to ask this question so that it'll come out right. But what I'm wondering is—is there no way for us to find a solution without sending Pop away?

Arnie: *(after a beat)* I'm with Uncle Warren, Dad. I was just thinking as I was filling the car. It really doesn't seem right to kick Grandpa out when we have the whole other side of the house for him to live in.

M. Sue: I'll help Mother better.

Lewis: *(taking it all in, looks at Bobby)* Don't you have anything to say, Bobby?

Bobby: *(not quite sure of himself)* I just want us all to be happy.

Charles: *(after a tense pause)* Now you all listen to me for a moment. Let's get hold of ourselves. This is not a tragedy—we're all going to be happy. You all stand there and look at me as though I'm dying. Well, I'm not dead yet, I'll tell you that, not by a long shot. I plan to live long enough to see Arnie's children and, if God spares me, maybe even their children too. Now quit looking at me as though I'm some old invalid who's just about to croak. I'm moving to Golden Hills, which isn't very far away, and I'll come to see you and you'll come to see me. Now let's all shut up, help carry things, and get in the car. Come on, let's go. *(Arnie and Warren head out.)* Come on, Bobby, get on over there and carry my suitcase. Margaret Sue, what are you waiting for? *(They go out and, as he goes to follow them, Esther stops him.)*

Esther: *(tone uncertain, strained)* Pop, I think maybe it's better if I don't go along. *(glancing at Lewis, then back to Charles)* I'll come see you soon.

Charles: *(turning)* That's fine, Esther. *(with warmth)* You take care of yourself.

Esther: I was just thinking, Lewis, next Saturday's the big game, and maybe we could invite Pop home here for lunch so he could go along to the game.

Lewis: I like that idea.

Charles: Thanks, Esther. It's a date. Of course, I should warn Arnie that I'll have to start routing for the Bears now that they'll be my home team! *(They chuckle.)* Goodbye, Esther.

Esther: Goodbye, Pop. *(He turns to go, then pauses, turns, and strides back to grip her hand in a fervent handshake.)*

Charles: *(fighting emotion, his voice is strong and full of feeling)* God bless you, Esther. You're a good woman!

Esther: *(hugging him impulsively, fighting tears)* I'm sorry, Pop, I'm so sorry. *(He hugs her for a moment, then pulls back his hand on her arm as he looks her right in the eye.)*

Charles: It's okay, Esther, it's okay. *(He looks at her, trying to smile, then turns and strides downstage right, pausing before he exits to turn and survey the room one last time.)*

Esther: I'll come see you soon, Pop.

Charles: *(nodding)* Thanks for everything, Esther. Even the squirting grapefruit! *(He chuckles, then turns and goes out. Lewis and Esther watch for a moment. Then Esther speaks.)*

Esther: *(with tears in her voice.)* I'll miss that man.

Lewis: *(walking close to her)* You sure you don't want to come along? *(Phone rings)*

Esther: No, you go. I'll be waiting for you. *(They embrace each other, the phone still ringing.)* I'll get the phone.

Lewis: I'll be back soon. *(He crosses and exits.)*

Esther: *(answering the phone)* Hello. Hi, Mother. How are you? How's Dad? What? Is he hurt? Which hospital is he in? *(Her tone is cautious.)* No, we'd love to have you come and stay here a few days. . . .

(CURTAIN)

About the Author

Merle Good has authored numerous plays and books. His first novel, *Happy as the Grass Was Green*, was produced as the movie *Hazel's People*, starring Geraldine Page and Pat Hingle.

TODAY POP GOES HOME has enjoyed wide acceptance and numerous productions, both in community theater productions as well as in educational settings.

He and his wife Phyllis live in Lancaster, PA, with their two daughters.